# Failure's Finest Moment

**Brian VanRemmen**

Published 2019 by Coyote Blood Press

*Failure's Finest Moment.*
Copyright 2018 by Hip Pocket Books.
ISBN: 9781090355690

Please direct inquiries to the author, attn:
Brian VanRemmen, bvanr@yahoo.com
Twitter: @AardvarkBV
Instragram @aardvark1979

Cover photo and art & "Broken Booth" photo by Chris Wise

# ACKNOWLEDGMENTS

The author(s) of this book would not be possible without the following entities: highly influentials Brian McMahon, Michael Demyan, Eric P. Johnt, HP Murphy, Ryan Buynak, Eric Gelsinger, Matt Proctor, Ian Belknap, John Knapp, Constance Renfrow, Ryan Drag, Craig Kite, Lucas Hunt, Bradley Lastname, Robert Pomerhn, Felix Buchloh, Jared Shapiro, Gregory and Maria VanRemmen, Ryan and Welles VanRemmen, Mom and Pop VanRemmen, Dan'l Bair, Joe Boz, Biff, Thomas J. Carloni, Air Force, Dorian Gray Tap & Grill, and the members of Blackhorse RFC, Village Lions RFC, Skippy Lizards, Washington RFC, Buffalo Old Boys RFC.

This book would not be possible without the endless love and support of my wife, Tanya Fazal, for whom I am ever grateful. The most special thank you, I love you and Baby Taira too! #Frogvark

"Corruption of the Sky" and "Race of Patriots" were previously published in DenimSkin #5.

# CONTENTS

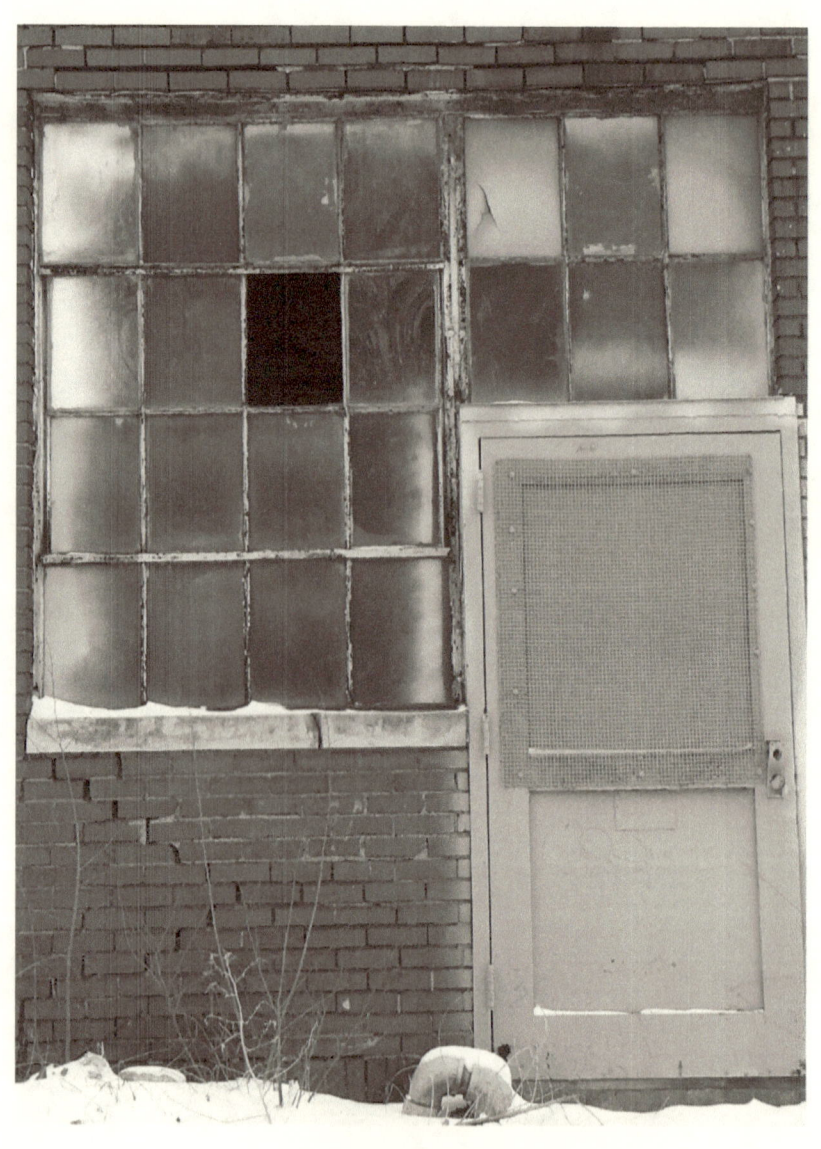

**CHAPTER 1: ENTRANCE**

**Birthday Poem**

The carnival
ceases.
The clowns
collapse
tents down,

ring toss
and fish tanks
dismantled,
handed over one
by one
into old Chevys
and Fords—

the bearded lady
skipped town
but returned with casks of wine.

The midgets
are already drunk.

Asphalt
stained by cotton
candy
and trailer tracks.

A gap-toothed
gamesman
takes a smoke
break.

The ring leader
swims by
saying,

"Get inside!
there's a thunderstorm a-comin'
and I don't want
any of you cursed things
getting struck by
lightnin'!"

Perch Poem


Macabre mind
in dusk-hollow
        day    carved sunless
           by scaffolds    stretched
                to sky,

    brick upon
           piled brick.

Sharp light
        breaks
        straight
            for ground—

   in silhouette
an old woman
hunched
    in her garden sighs.

The hot dog stand
           is the last outpost

    of capitalism.

Every syllable
    a strange
    laugh    then silence,
           a stone rolling
    over
wrinkled trousers.

      The mail
     arrives
        Bukowski style,

    the nude descends the stairs.

What to Load

Have   you     loaded
                    the soundtrack
                                        to your light-year leap
                                                for a ride
                                                    all the way
                                                    to the sun?

Anticipation builds
                                an emergency bursts,
      but you'll be attended to—
                            the birds
                                    will bear   you safely.

Even in   this giant's
                            age
                        we                      drive     55—

someone should use
                    my   height
                            to make

                                                    a movie.

I've a   confidence
                    that's     king—

                                    I can't                    keep it
in.

                    Everything that belongs
      is packed,
                        locked
                            and stepped,
                                        ready

                                                to roll.

13

## From an RV Looking East

Back window of a beat-up pickup,
muffler hung with coat hanger
duct taped to rear end,
watching our tread extend
across Kansas
and all that came before.

Blue skies back east,
and our former lives,
flint fields
west of both Manhattans—

on this ride every thought
is racing toward a
lone
homeless heaven heaved
through time zones.

Strangers
at every angle incredible,

soft spaces
between places
where friends await—
            dormers or ditch diggers—

a calloused handshake
extending
the memory thread
across endless,
interminable miles

made bearable by
arrival's exiled smiles.

**Premeditated Immersion in Immediacy**


This is not
      the final way
words
         will be conveyed,

from discovery to design
transitioned to your table,
enabling
my mind.

Trust me
when I say
I planned it.

But what
is this
plain poem?

Perhaps
leave this space
alone.

         A chance for something magical—
         this is why the game is played.

Entropic
boundaries.

Too tired to try,
in a panic
of irrelevancy.

Endless variant,
auto pretend,
locked and step,
a breakaway.

## Divine Traveler, Parch Your Wet Throat

Empty the breakfast tray,
send the maid away.

Anthologize yourself
to antagonize    the    process.

Knowledge in every syllable,
energy churns
a thousand miles from home.

Go fry an egg.
Get an office
made in my image
like nine batters lined
up at spring training.

I got drunk
and rode my voice hoarse.

Yeah, stranger, go yogi.
Go rollin' in rickshaw in reverse—
give the driver a ride.

Heap hot coals round your soles,
trample the smoldering image-makers,
gladiator language rankers.

Curious times to let words fly,
censured by verse-burglars
insisting I couldn't handle the worst.

But my voice is fast approaching
and even eons of the world's wisdom
can never, never slake this thirst.

Asking the House


Take a good look
at the work
that consumes the week,
and then what gets one by—

I have a roof but I'm asking

                          the house.

               Since when is the blueprint followed?

     Even a spectacle perfectly produced
                won't provide—
compelled to do something
                    on the side.

Don't divide or even chop,
       no matter how mangled.

Let me keep my hands, blistered,
scarred—
splayed out.

To speak for me from rooftops,
corridors, clandestine closet
ground floor,
         elevators
hauling me through high rises.

Hold me no longer,     I     will     not     hide.

It's high time
to kick out the walls
       and follow the wandering light.

## Thousand Wood Windows

Before the first step
    calculate
    force needed for movement,
    to coordinate the leap—
        a physical arrival,
parenthetical weave.

The way one covers a bald spot,
    a pattern inside the gap.

It all comes out in a breath.

You could live without fingers
but for language that is death.

                This poem of thumbs.

    A mind unraveling
in heedless exploration

        from eyeball
            to neuron
                    to mark
                        on the page.

The feeling rises.
Like blood to hips or breath to lips

    it's coming, it's coming
      out the fingertips—

    stumped up from ground
    like some organ out of control,

      a natural sensation        of organic
                organization.

Lines on hands
    capture serious lineage,

a great forest exterminated in degrees.

But what deal is in the reveal?
Can we burn to dust
the life we steal?

In dimensions of darkness
where all corners round,

avoid
       turns
               until all steps are static.

Better integrate energy
into language loaded,
    handled with care,
a shared syntax
    passed like glass packed with reefer
                   (whatever you prefer),

        this breath
        can't be steered.

There is no objection
    to    a way    of speaking.

    Conversation carried in
  the open space of vowels,

darkness
        framed        and formless,

    death at constant end.

Jersey Barrier

At the window
with clouds and cliffs
and white birds
in swamps,

the smeared faces
laughing at an actual past,

        not some projected future.

Beaches made mirthful
by footprints
and the tide hushed to sleep.

Daydream in traffic
on the turnpike,
build a garden courageously
in the median.

A mechanical mystery
wrecks
reality
as all humanity
rubber necks
at an overturned
truck.

No dry eyes in this house.

An unforgiving wind
destroys the joy
in Jersey—

no cliffs,
no clouds,
no birds.

## Caesar in a Brutal Meeting

*"Among so much good we tamped down the crime." – John Berryman*

Pride suffers wounds
      worse than any bone
                       or muscle,

a struggle under robes
      unbeknownst
              to underlings

armed with knives
              for a fight.

No agendas, appointments—

steel in the back
                    or stick in the eye,
      justice trimmed of fat.

Accept the fate.

Anticipate
        the look.

    Trust to die
in tragedy,

      busted descending
   the devil's staircase,

a climate ripe for riot.

Exhaled breath—
        the signal.

Daggers out
       to silence the sage,

minions to center
suddenly
               swarm.

Historic contrition,
       a tunic torn—

all crime committed
          to memory
      is best left
            to the page.

# 30 Year Ruminations

The chill
    tempers the thrill of turning 30,
        this January
            it stands to reason
    that age will soon beat beauty.

I dreamed of
        big guitars
      and bigger cars,
    steak and scotch
           sitting at the bar,

I'm unwelcome
    in the clubs downtown.

    Freedom
      is a half-life,
    carbon can't date me.

      I need flesh and blood.

Embrace
a decade of waking in a race.
    A sleeping chase.

I've asked life
  what to do,
and I've thirty years
to get at it.

      But I can't buy
        what isn't mine

and I'm decades yet
    from dying.

**Send Off Paull Young**

The company
I've kept
keeps me poking
the abyss,

probing
through space
                    exposed
like an accent
on a pop kick.

The man
could sell
ivory to elephants.

There's a charity
smuggling
smug laughs
under sweaters
in San Francisco.

Send me
a postcard
of a lizard
on a lion
climbing the golden gate.

'Til next
we have beers together,
it will be
too long
a wait.

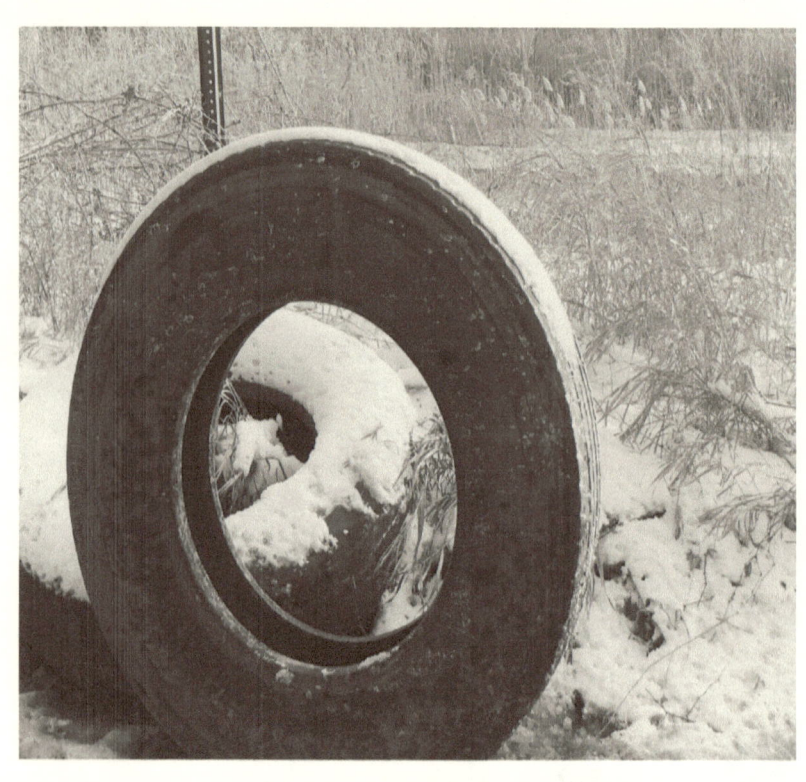

**CHAPTER 2: DEFUNCT CIRCULAR**

**Tracing the Waterline**


All the snowmen melt at once,
      I'm up to my nose in carrots.

I rewrote rules and
               spoke sentences          when I needed a light.

Fire melted memory.

A rowboat burned
between shoreline and cliff.

Stones get bigger and sharper.
             The hard stones
snigger at the big alone.

            Sand in solidarity.
Signatures at high-water,
points between the lines.

Hand the world
             to the right man,

to love the curves and soft parts.

           [soft parts]                [hard parts]


Barge into the unknown—
               corner turn,
                    corner encounter.

Warning unheard.

                Still, working hard
                    to listen loud.

The Leap

Experience
constant change.

Learn
from mistakes.

Choose fight.

Break that
campaign trail
gripping town to town.

Never
          is a strong word
                    in a world of swords.

Choose flight.

Chalk it up
   to traded licks
                    and glass handshakes.

Come back
                              zoned,

          commercial
                                   retail

                    stale on change,

                         long on experience,

     embedded in brick cliffs
          chipped from beef cities.

                    I swoon at a good speech.

**Snowy Surface**

This time:
                    a bullet point
                    big explosion,
                    a happy accident,
                    dog's best friend.

Did this poem growl to life
        where dishes do their duty?

Duck now, watch the step.
                              Down not out, do it now!

        Add it up.                    Go ahead.
                    Actions at least loud.

It smells like snow,
        but   snow   is slowly    past it's prime—
move it or melt it,
no stopping time.

Fuck later, nothing comes
                              from nothing—
            don't anticipate,
                    participate.

Announce and salute.
Articulate the sum of the parts,
                                        right there.

The flag you wave
                is falling
                    note    by
                              note
                                    by
                                        note
                                        like snow.

**As I Am**

**Mississippi burial mounds
tell**
> **tall,**

> > **strange       tales.**

**Badlands trampled,
bejeweled beaks on Bowery**

> > **bump flat-brimmed ball caps in Omaha.**

> **The perfect gaze
gassed out on avenues—**

**too many plans
> makes a man
> > familiar**

> > **with failure.**

**Footsteps
rearrange
> the giggle,
a day
> sensing
> for            a difference.**

**Unsteady
> directly,
> > the intention
> > > must be true.**

The Strange Familiar

Like brushes on snares,
          unaware

of the strange scent
          of familiar air.

The year turns
          and the tambourine rattles
          off-beat.

We wake
          to chase
                    the dream
          again today,

when there is no place we're going.

Out of the ordinary
          into the fray,

use a stone
to say
          something softly.

Always opportunity,
boundless and beginning,

light older than diamonds
          doubling as chalk.

# Map the Alone

Shoulder the door
      to the heart
              shut.

Shudder at the visage
      in glass
            gleaming

      middle-class mobility.

            Pay attention to the beat,
                the street,
drive the wrong way home.

            [How does he know where home is?]

Train the trail to match footstep,
      everyday urban ramble
            hemmed by crosswalks
        on concrete,
            sign posts,
                streetlights,
                even air is gated—

    metal detectors
        decode DNA.

Heart beat    is      ir        i      ir      reg  u    lar,
                      bring a doctor in,
    streets
e      x      p      a      n      d      i    n      g

Home is no home.

Even maintenance men

                                    are        lost,

supervisors relent,

"Here,

                    [Hands me a pitchfork]

                                    guard the door alone."

Burn down those rubber soles,
        get that soul black.

## Influenza (33 Februaries)

Wisdom is bound to create
    demons, crutches,
        vices to hate—

a heart and a head
can lock the vault
    but out there it's madness—
        rein yourself to fate.

Every safe house
    penetrable,
        no cave can save.

Really, it's sickness,

    a twist on the business,
      a risk to living,
    a loaded pistol.

We're all nutritious—
    the saintly,
        the knave.

But digging up
        a beggar's ditch
    will send you to the grave.

## Stacked Gap

A table tips
    under heavy load
into sharks' mouths.
A circling reward.

    I've a code
    to hold the bullies back,
a broken pipe
no one
wants to use,

    a jester's sneer
      belies the gripe—

the fools
    are kings of every stripe.

Though bull horns holler
behind barricades
    the hammer heads
      rush in,
a serenade
    shocked silent
playing shell games
    with our skin.

        The rocks come flying through the windows
        Ha! Hurrah!
        The rocks come flying through the windows
        Ha! Hurrah!
        The rocks are flying, head's a-roll
        Gravity takes back all control
        Ha! Hurrah! Hurrah!

The Era of Surreal Politics


Talk to mad-hatted
                    mayhem makers—

the mortality
                    of this democratic mess

        depends
                    on arbitrary handshakes.

Our savior
                    is ordinary,
                            salvation                    unstable,

                    a confusion refused.

It is a new age of poems.

A voice
                    in all epochs.

Let the era
                            engage
            in unconditional
                                    olive branch

        extensions.

The future
                    contradictory,

                                            a web
                                            wherein
                                            we're  meant
                                            to be.

Blockbuster

Answer the bell
to shill on streets again,
          this time it's your life.

Called to be everywhere  at once,
unfinished epiphanies
under the arm.

Fill the seats
with daylight,
stream sunshine
in from wings.

Light up this house
from beginning     to end,
leave in disbelief.

It's time to make mountains.

Stretch shoulders
to bear the weight                    of words.

It will be the last time
the note is read.
Have it once or never.

Circle
in endless
                    aimlessness,
acting
in accordance
with the laws of will,

the play of fools,
but never
the same game.

## Massed Media

Surely it's a mistake
to consume the caffeine
of the American dream.

What do you mean
I'm swimming upstream?

This time it's personal,
families involved.

A single son
on which this story revolves.

Clenched in fist
an emptiness
begs for
confession.

We are waiting,
standing still.

We are waiting
for the world
to return.

A voice suspended,
static in the air,

silence like a siren—

easy
to ignore.

## Little Town

A hard day
and great date through,
an evening of bliss—

on a raggedy avenue
our first deep kiss,
perfunctory but perfect,

a hand-held balance
on a spinning star,
an encounter not to miss.

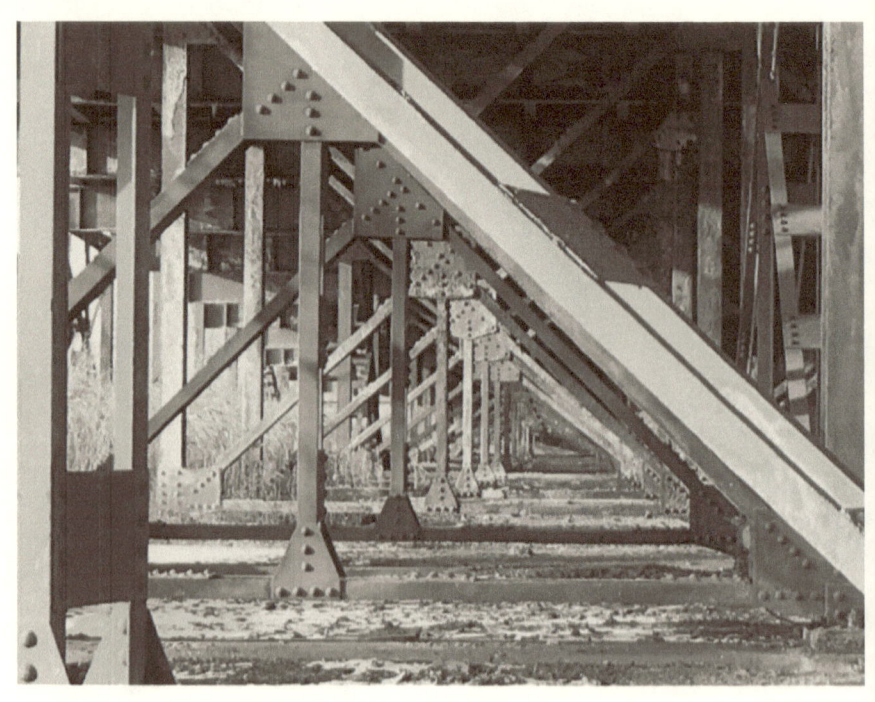

# CHAPTER 3: GIRDERS

**Hiding in the Henhouse**

Wind
          swept
                    stench
                              through Harlem streets,

     soft feathers
          swirl
     on bodega boys
               bemoaning
               lack of greatness
               at bottle's
                         bottom.

Thugs protecting
     hormone drugs,

               parolees on patrol.

Henchmen
cage yard

                    stiff

upper lip—

roost ruler
               solitary

     in penthouse.

Better a devil
     than extra
in this
                    cosmic
                         movie,

extend
slender finger

into cauldrons
of time.

Lukewarm responses
to tremendous
crises

tempt society
to embrace
the chase,

an endless race,

better
than the curse
of a cage.

Wrong Holiday


Whispers get louder—
        a fever, it's the flu.

      Investigate the whole picture—
      parts are blown up pixels,
      luggage in the air.

Courage won't work anymore.

    Worries have
                lost the war,

    no battle remains
             but rage
on all fronts.

      Growth stunted
    like planks on a rotten bridge, stomped on
      and tumbling—

      we are
             in the river,
we are                 in the lake.

             No boat ever floated this far.


      Not even mud suckers
and helicopters can get me.

I'm nothing, never there.

      The soft air addictive,
        a precipice
of gallantly,
    a fine place to frolic,
    perfect to prance.

**Barefoot Man**

The best bears
            forage in dumpsters

but when humans stoop
            to animal craving,

the savings and
                loan
                    can't bail us out.

We live by excuses
and half-truths

        blunted by
            fatigue.

Bruises
      migrate,

           the buses

     integrate.

Are we grateful
        for houses,
                  for heat—

                 that we can pay
                    for what we eat?

 The dark breeds
desires
          that are not ours.

**Fuse confusion!**

**The fire is**
        **a man**
                    **on stage**
                **railing**
        **against short hoses**

                            **—dies shirtless in an alley.**


**Catastrophe**

    **is**
        **failure's**

        **finest**

        **moment.**

Unfit

Find me a word
            that isn't fit to print
to hit on the head again.

            I'm done, I'm it.

This fool thought
bamboo school
            was best
but I can't go back
and correct.

The vibrato swings
            in the wind
                        like a ditched dick—

a hammer thrown to the dome
brings the poem home.

            Some bullies took my lunch box
            playboy history book.

I'm chewing the nerves
            raw and bloody,
                        scarred lips reach
            for the alpha's
                        meat,

            beefs
                        are best fought
                        with fists.

**Truth in Action**

Heart

                              —vulnerable to weather
                              & delicate instruments


               keeps
          the dream
     for the          dreamer.

Passion picks
   reality,

self-thought
                         shipwrecks

stuck
on reefs
          the way
                    vision
                         picks
                              out
                                   freaks


          on open plain.

**These Movies**


Do not shock.
Bread
is more shocking.

      Do you think
      this is just
      for you?

The spinning reels
make more in a day
than I'll see
in a lifetime

but this
is no
complaint.

I'm full
of agility,

flexible
as yoga pants
on flat asses.

What we see
on screen is stiff
as board.

I've been given
the gift of dream,
and nothing
the guards
or dogs
can do
will stop
them from reaching you.

## Race of Patriots

On the corner
      holding details down,
      with green backs
                and plastic
      we don't swim,
                      we drown.

The dock, the desk, register.
      Dreaming
           on a string.

      Everything a world away,
      a theme you cannot say.

Knowledge and power
      in the hands
           of few—
   where protocols      are compromised,
      no one knows what to do.

Paranoia, indecision,
      the ruse
           on TV news.

      Protest bullhorns, silent tweets—
      but none connect the clues.

See no evil, hear no truth,
      steel yourself
for more abuse.

# Hero Training (Or, How to Become an Emperor)

We both rode
tricycles
in high
Sierra
towns,

after the mayhem
of skids
in frog socks
on hardwood floors.

                    Why did you fall up?

                                     It's one thing
                                     to defy logic,

      but gravity too?

We'll kick
          out
     a one-eyed jack
     to smack
             you into shape,
pinch

     through a crack in the eyeball.

Play some records
or a real guitar,
     follow scratches
          to capture
     a batch of tears
in a bottle.

Going
       inward
is no way
to ride a bike.

Push toward panic,
aware of all snares.

Erase the itch.
Delay the craze.

Wander
      with a party gardener's tools,

hidden,

forbidden,
      on last legs

grooving above witnesses,

     nerves fraying
             on the wheel.

# The Break Out

Take a drag on the lighted night,
    the one to which
                      you escape
     when you churn out
     hidden secrets,

          outside the long eye
          of prying corporate spies
          or narrow-minded miners
          of self-worth.

No matter how you sex it up
                  no healthy glow appears.

             This year failure writes all over.

Demons can follow
    so don't drag the feelings.

                  Lock the doors.

             The chains
                        will hang you

    soon enough.

Reverse it—

  let the guilt get out.

     Sweep it up with stasis.

                  Your freedom

   always breathes.

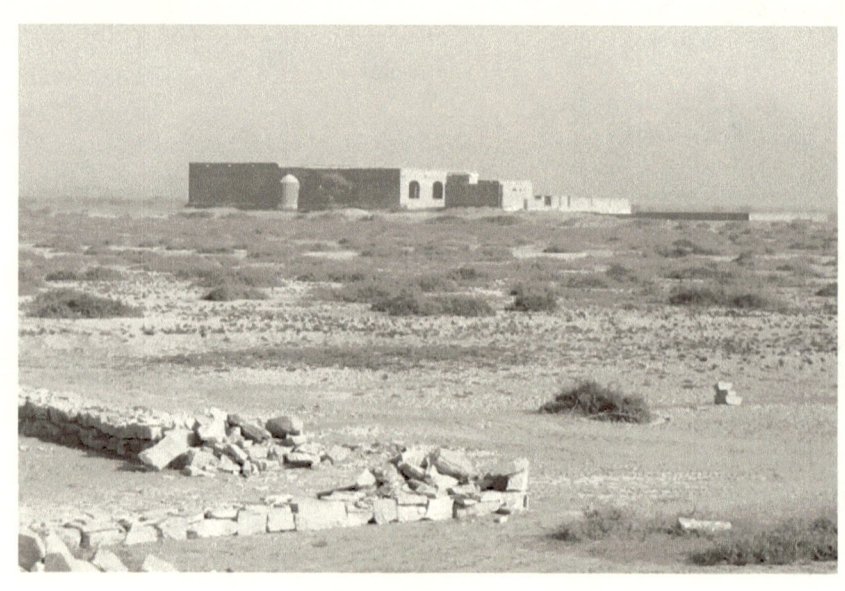

**CHAPTER 4: A LIKELY FUTURE**

Independence


Silence
the wavers
of star-spangled flags,
stand them down
to sit
		this one

					out.

Ask yourself
some questions
without speaking
to a machine.

This is literal,
I see it
on repeat.

Accusing me of truth?

To be strong
and brave
is to be
a little insane.

Sound off
to stir the static—
				once you shout
			words
they cannot
			be said
				again.

Listen close
to hear
freedom
ring.

Sahara Wind


I'm shackled to a Sahara wind,
    forgotten the way a desert forgets.

        Endless sameness never the same.

    This cracked land crawled
    to an oasis
        of time-lapse
            performance space,

      a place where schemes are hatched.

Remain motionless
    for long enough
  you're an easy target
        for rocks.

It's tendencies
    from childhood
  that make us eternal.

A road
of knuckled turns,

  a roaring caravan
      of thought.

The horn of Africa, Thebes,
    observatory of the Freedom Tower
           over endless,
        never-the-same island,

  a millennium of deserts
obscuring the view.

**Wheels through the Windshield**

I am
      chopped up
      chipped away
            cheated on
            choked out.

The whiners
              dine
with fame-seeking
            dream breakers,
            edifice makers,
            ego shakers
                      all the time.

What's in now
      that can't become?

            Too many beats,
            not enough drums.

      Tiptoes
            and tie-downs,
      a future
of found sound.

Each bound breath
      pulled random from the queue,

imagination's
      heresy,

            the unfortunate accident
      to know the future
            in advance.

**Corruption of the Sky**


**Our bubble**
        **is built**

        **on networks**
        **of newsworthy**
                        **items**
        **in nondescript days.**

        **What we think is fleeting**
        **is instant,**
        **the same.**

**Seeking**
      **is obsession,**

       **aggressive expectations**
                           **unachieved.**


                **Eat**
    **at the wheel of cheese**
    **but   it  may not please**
    **and is not free.**

**The shark has swum for eons,**
    **kicks are never brave.**

    **Fame is a notion.**
        **Language but a wave.**

**Word Doctors**

There's a dude
with Doc Martens
across
from me
on the subway.

I swear he's
using me
to write.

Does he know
I also state
what I
mean
to say?

We are
moving
on similar
means
but lack
a method
to arrive.

Thieve
these shouts, sir,
if you ever
need a place.

Free
for reckless
abandon,

to never
be used
again.

# Spring, New York City

It's crusty black
ice snow,
layered.

New flakes landing
on thirsty earth,
morning,
dry
where once
there was
a river.

Spring   is
past springs
remembered
    inexactly,
memory
believes
already
it's arrived.

This day
years ago
it rained.

A season
of beginnings
starts harder
than salt piles
on pavement
crunching
under
my boot,

the sound
of melting snow.

## Capture a Snapshot in a Moment That Is Now

Hustling down
dark Bed-Stuy streets
        under rattling signs,

endless avenue
        south    to sand    then sea.
    With ghostly
        cigarette hacks
            behind me,
    shadows
        of failed dates
            falling on my failed state,

where's comfort   promised?

If I duck in doorways
    or crush cans with flesh fulfilled,
        my number is called,

                                then a dash.
It's a thrill to love
        but no fun    to eat    the kill.

Charge every chance
    with action,
an act        done only now.

I've the will
    and clarity
      to not
        choose a side—

                            alone,
        unteachable,

          making moments,

      making.

**Undesign**

Identified by what I lack,
undefined by design,

I rack up violations
with no plan to pay the fine.

Vision revised
      coloring outside lines.

A miracle
of casting calls
for tragic irrationality,
a comedian by trade
is most in tune
with reality.

              I've a new partner now,
                       one without a name—

    a gypsy misfit,

                  some thing to not be seen.

In China Camp shrimp pits
hold forth     in holds    of slave ships,

     don't miss the mythical.
     Imagination skips.

        Lay an egg, hatch an epic,
        make a mermaid.

They're under the viaduct    on Austin Street,
       a god's design
              incomplete.

**Easter Fools**


A guy
hauls a bag
dripping
red liquid

all over subway seats,

screaming
he bears
the blood
of the Lord.

Looks like
Hawaiian Punch
to me.

There's a teenager
with stigmata,
an old man in a robe.

Is this
the ensemble cast
of the Bible's
black comedy
or just a train
Brooklyn bound
on the evening commute?

Still the man
insists he's heading
to heaven
via 8th avenue express,

carrying
credentials
for everlasting life.

**Strange Place of My Past**

The chances
I pass up
are past due.

Someone
to come
will collect.

The demand
for default
an assault
on sensible
thought.

Think the last
generation
had such ideas?

Generate
energy
and bills
pile up.

Lists
get
longer.

The heat
gets
to me.

I have to go
into circles
of strange men.

It's pathological
biology,

the match stick's
chance strike
at reality.

Aberration,

I am
mutation's
cold soul.

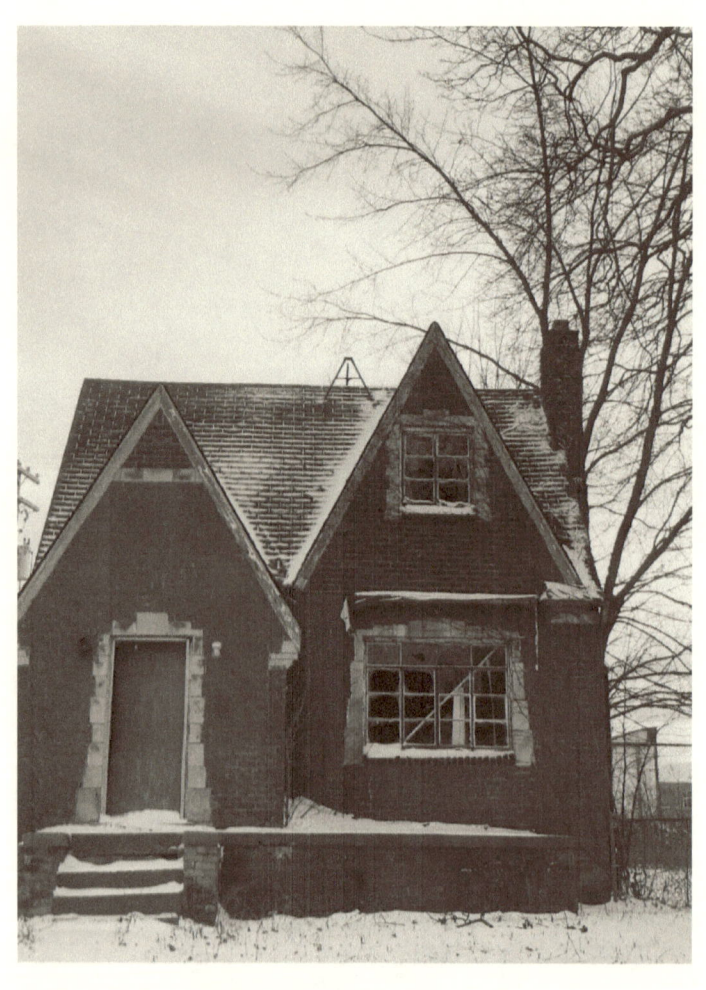

**CHAPTER 5: EMPTY EMPIRES**

No New Fire


When the house
caught fire
a strange thing
happened.

We escaped
to the sidewalk,
stood
to watch
the conflagration.
Secretly
I hoped
it would burn
to foundation.

Suddenly the fire
extinguished.
It ran
                                    out
of oxygen,
exhausted
it's fuel.

After that
no light came
to the house.

No fire
ever burned.

In cold darkness
we lived
the rest
of our lives.

**Upper Hudson Sketch**

Some strange depot
      for the soul     is out here,

an outpost of  gold  red  green
                          at the outer ends
      of a hundred million trunks.

The roots,
      grounded,    thirsty,
               fuel me.

A disguise donned
           for professional
              purposes   discarded.

Deep cuts
   in Champlain's cliffs
            do not debilitate.

Pure
thoughts of love
           for one woman
                  and all mankind
     ring
         down
   the mountain side,

      dip head under
          a tumbling stream,

     reborn
     by colors
     of decay.

## Left in Woods


They junked that truck      in '86
              after the carburetor went.

My uncle steered it off the ledge.
      All the cousins pushed.

The embankment
      made the axles rattle.
Squirrels scattered.
             We heard the windshield shatter.

      Steel rusted and rubber thinned,
a drifter
      took the radio,

             an artifact
                      into    ether.

The skeleton weathered
chaos and crisis,
crashes and calm.

When I was told
          to do
             what I've always done,

I took
      the cable box and DVDs,
        credit cards and color TV,
          radio and remote control,

went to the woods
      with the obsolete goods,
        tossed 'em to the truck
        and never gave another fuck.

# Not Where Bodies Are Buried, but Where Skeletons Lie

Have a look inside
    the closet of your mind,
even in strange times
    we have our oldest friends.

No matter your tribe
    or the stripes on your socks
        those who come closest
        fall farthest back.

Stretched and dead like empty streets
    in suburb alleys of vinyl fence,

as far back as you dare,
                dig it up,
                but be aware.

            The grins
        cannot be wiped.

These old bones
    make us,
    like clothes we keep
    or words we speak.

Bring them out warily,
            once,
                  for all—

    it's the last party,
    a chance to make
    the most interesting thing happen
    then die a brutal death.

## Here's a Thought

There are people
born of people.
From people ideas flow,
of the people
one and all.

As marginal waves
from rivers
ideas endless,
thoughts
for better ideas,
rivulets of thought
from people
form rivers,
ideas flow.

Oceans
of thought
overflowing,
so many
thoughts
by people
over take
ideas,
now marginal.

Ideas
from people,
marginal,
thoughts
marginal,
ideas old,
thought gone,
people
drowned
in thought.

## Sunday Driver #9

What's ecstatic
                fits
my world.
But this world
shrinks.

Car is fast
rhythm fast
action faster.

Pull the brakes on the moment.

Once stopped
hit the jets
off interstate exit,

the curve        collapsing     on my neck.

Extend the day
deedless
to noises
of kazoos
in traffic.

Being born turns the key.

Once you twist   on
     there is          no off
until that fucker dies.

This whole bucket is a secret,

yet here we are,
perched on the horizon
running
for the edge.

**Muscle**

I've become
flexible
suddenly                                        (at least up here).

It contributes
to erasure
of time
restrictions,
picks up
through rightness
of worlds.

No mother        nature
madness
for me.

I'll face the pull
of laziness,
make it my scapegoat.

Lead smartly.
                    There are obstacles.

Large chunks
of me may die.

Activate
what was once
anticipation,
and act away.

What's left
is sinewy
and sly—
substance
over style.

# The Black Throat

Moving from city
to country
on asphalt badland,

        sand bagging
        for rainy days ahead,

pockmarked
pathways
through the nation,
        no arteries these.

Recent history proves
if there's facts available,
        take an alternate route.

Compose lonesome blues
        in space
of what we know,

what we're told
between exits
means nothing.

We must pound
this pavement,
cracking codes
in cracks,

hard study
the potholes
til head hurts,

use eyes
to learn
as well as to see.

If it is real
where rubber
meets road,
                    rearrange.

These highways
take courage
to drive.

Be reckless
around curves,

cut off
the directionless.

Enter interior
on interstates
running reverse
'cross causeways,

something sensible,
sensitive.

Emboldened
to exorcise
what's deep in the soul,

when all we know
is here at home.

Easy

More than fame
itself,
fans are trapped.

Cubicle kids
catfishing
celebrities
keep reality's
mantle
on the front foot.

To admit
reach
is to appear
weak.

Neurons tell
the heart
to waste
a beat.

It's worth nothing
to be known,
yet
we all
want it.

Famously
naïve,
a network
of neat
little lives,

an imagination
dulled,
wit obscene.

Spouting Drivel

Hear that
automated voice
say Spuyten—

                              drivel?

A whole lot of nothing.

Imagine being filled
                                    with it.

Full of things

          you can't understand?

That voice.

It's not
how it's said
but what
the words are.

                    All the words.

I heard them.

They ask
for things
we cannot provide,

directions
for destinations
that don't exist.

Inaccessible
by foot
       or fearlessness.

                         There's a scary thought.

But a world
without words
              is terrifying.

                         Unimaginable.

I wish
we were here

              already

but wishes
get us

         nowhere.

## Sunday Rider

There are former
minds
I want to go back to—

a little wing
will get me there.

Perhaps
the subway
sway
is best
of all.

Naked
in an empty car
            in my head.

It's all
in movement,
the road    or rail
beneath
sneaky glances
passed
to strangers,

crooked
in all entrances.

Foot beat is freedom,
obscenity to boot.

Sounding off
for substance,
                        calling
for the business end
of the blues.

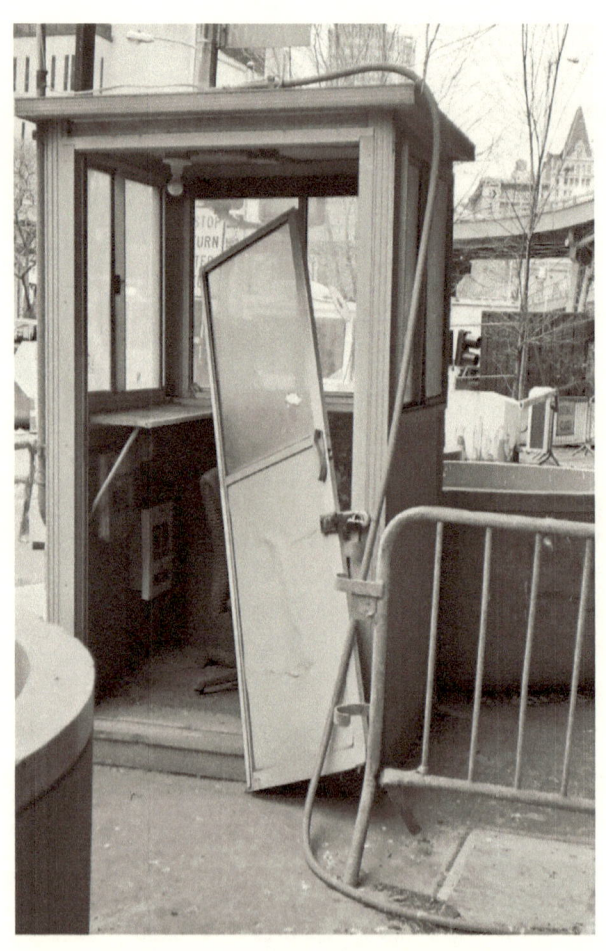

**CHAPTER 6: BROKEN BOOTH**

## Not to Be Revealed

There are secrets
I will take
to the grave.
So dark
not even the page
can save.

So deep
not even drugs
can excite
lips
to talk,

no mouth
to form
lewd stories
of lustful
misadventure
with beginning,
middle,
and longer middle.

All rules
on me

I placed
myself.

Nothing
held onto.

Passages
traced
cannot
be navigated
forever.

My borders
are open
frontier.

I'm entitled
to life
and that's it.

Preserve these
words

an edifice
burns.

In immortality,
secrets
revealed.

## Natural Causes

The delta
in this equation
is our distance
from the storm
forming
off to the west,

an ominous
orange
at front edge,

electric
explosions
absent
emotion,

announcing entry
in a fanfare
of heavy cloud
and heavenly coolness,

celestial compounds
cling
to hot air,

harboring
no ill will,

headed
straight
for us.

## Whirly Pop Colors

I don't know
what the barcode
signifies
but I'm sure
it is
delicious.

Ice
liquidated
on tongue.

Anxiety
released
in a lick.

Being bought
and sold
has advantages.

Like selling
rainbows
to leprechauns,

to be footloose
in a freezer

is what's wanted
all along.

Motivator


Confusion
begets
the overwhelming
anger.
I want out.

I will not worship.
I will not judge.

I build my house
from brick and mud,
no fancy
chandeliers.

Even my greatest hits collected
only squeak by.

But my mute
prayers
to no one are free,
nothing
has no price.

What I make
is all ours,
my method in your head.

I'll keep
your secrets,
speak in repeats,
sing silent
for streetlights,
sweating
sweet psalms
into the palace
of these palms.

Swinging


Unanswered
like old men
in the park
barking orders
to an old platoon,

none of us
conduct
attention
long enough.

Decisions forced
to support a self
on cheap plastic,
chain link
and steel.

One cannot question
the object
if one
wants
to fly.

No more ambiguity
                              on stage,
rearrange approaches
to a landing patch.

Lead discourse
deliberately
from dirt,

momentum
draws feet
to sky.

**Defeating Rust**


What's
to lose?

These tools
are of my body
to be used
until ruined.

I would
do it all again,
strapped in
steady
to my destination.

Every sound
a siren.

Still
I'm hungry,

stunned
by what's
in range—

all
potential
possible.

Deep reach,
heart
beat,

centering
an unstoppable
force.

Escalator


Bounding down
escalators
is my everyday activity,
and under
a minute
in silence.

I'll leap
over standers
on the left,
uncompromising
climber
fast mover
begging forgiveness.

My goal
is to euthanize
funds, furious
stares fail.

There is dirt on everything,
at the top
a certain
center
of the speediest city,

it is what everyone wants.

At the apex
flip the switch,
atop a tower of stairs—

feeding
energy
ahead
to the next.

With Confidence


Everything in confidence
can be done
without consequence.

Burn anger
properly.
Certainty
in chance.

Build borders
with card board.

Put on
centers
of gravity
to motivate
the base.

Brutal
highways
and staircases
suddenly stopped
at the top.

Can't count cards
or roll loaded dice.

Still I ask,
with all the luck
in the world
at my back,

What's in it for me, man?
  What's in it for me?

Secret Weight

Do not put
the weight
of this visit to earth
under the heel of your foot.

Hold it
in the
chambers
of your heart.

It must all
be carried                    alone.

Best not to
relinquish control,
what is held is worth
the whole ton.
Bring it along
'til the eyes ache.

It will stay
all night
to loom
in dreams.

Let it burst into rooms breaking.

We can skip
on sidewalks
or miss
altogether,
but once there's land
to land on,
what's tucked
in deep
must never sleep.

## End Credits

We could be going to movies,
or moving.

Instead we watch TV,
we watch.

Carnage the same
            wherever we turn
the same.

I try to keep arm's length away,
I keep away.

The same song gets replayed
replayed, replayed.

I've been barking
            up lots of trees,
barking for days.

The fruit never falls
            in my yard,
never falls.

Always an accounting,
someone's counting.

Who will
pay the tab?

**Earth on the Line**

**Wait**

wait

wait

wait

wait

wait

wait

wait

wait

wait

wait

wait

wait

wait

wait.

**Too late.**

Everlasting


Perish
as dinosaurs did,
absconding
with all morality,

and go extinct.

Remember
the effort
it takes
to breathe.

Don't forget
it's sunlight
that makes us
survive.

Discard judgement
from daytime,

do not
get stuck
in mud.

The finest
of us—
fossils.

The lucky ones,
divine.

Born and raised in Buffalo, NY, Brian VanRemmen has been writing poetry for over twenty years. While balancing a full-time involvement in rugby with life as a cubicle jockey, writing poetry when he could, he cofounded Hip Pocket Books, a small independent press, in order to publish his own work and that of his community. His four previous poetry titles are *Notes from a Neophyte (Not a Manifesto)*, *The Optimist*, *Absurdity & Speed*, and *Temporary Author*. In NYC in 2013, Brian cofounded *DenimSkin*, a literary and art review, which published five issues consisting of poetry, black-and-white art and photography, short stories, and flash fiction. He appreciates the community of poets and artists in NYC and finds it essential to continue to work together to create, share, and celebrate each other's art, inspired by this great city.

www.ingramcontent.com/pod-product-compliance
Lightning Source LLC
Chambersburg PA
CBHW021848170526
45157CB00007B/2983